POPE FRANCIS

Candor Lucis æternæ

Apostolic Letter
on the Seventh Centenary
of the Death of Dante Alighieri

Cover Image:
Raphael (Raffaello Sanzio), *Il Parnaso*, Room of the Signatura, fresco, 1508-1511, detail
Photo © Governatorato S.C.V. - Direzione dei Musei

00120 Città del Vaticano
Tel. 06.698.45780
E-mail: commerciale.lev@spc.va

ISBN 978-88-266-0616-3

www.vatican.va

www.libreriaeditricevaticana.va

Splendour of Light Eternal, the Word of God became flesh from the Virgin Mary when, to the message of the angel, she responded: "Behold the handmaid of the Lord" (cf. *Lk* 1:38). The liturgical feast that celebrates this ineffable mystery held a special place in the life and work of the supreme poet Dante Alighieri, a prophet of hope and a witness to the innate yearning for the infinite present in the human heart. On this Solemnity of the Annunciation of the Lord, I readily add my voice to the great chorus of those who honour his memory in the year marking the seventh centenary of his death.

In Florence, which reckoned time *ab Incarnatione*, 25 March was the first day of the calendar year. Because of its closeness to the spring equinox and the Church's celebration of the paschal mysteries, the feast of the Annunciation was likewise associated with the creation of the world and the dawn of the new creation through the redemption won by Christ on the cross. It thus invites us to contemplate, in light of the Word made flesh, the loving plan that is the heart and inspiration of Dante's most famous work, the Divine Comedy, in whose final canto Saint Bernard celebrates the event of the incarnation in the memorable verses: "Within thy womb rekindled was the love, / By heat of which in the eternal peace / After such wise this flower has germinated" (*Par.* XXXIII, 7-9).*

Earlier, in the *Purgatorio*, Dante had depicted the scene of the Annunciation sculpted on a rocky crag (X, 34-37, 40-45).

On this anniversary, the voice of the Church can hardly be absent from the universal commemoration of the man and poet Dante Alighieri. Better than most, Dante knew how to express with poetic beauty the depth of the mystery of God and love. His poem, one of the highest expressions of human genius, was the fruit of a new and deeper inspiration, to which the poet referred in calling it: "the Poem Sacred / To which both heaven and earth have set their hand" (*Par.* XXV, 1-2).

* Trans. H. W. Longfellow (1867).

With this Apostolic Letter, I wish to join my Predecessors who honoured and extolled the poet Dante, particularly on the anniversaries of his birth or death, and to propose him anew for the consideration of the Church, the great body of the faithful, literary scholars, theologians and artists. I will briefly review those interventions, concentrating on the Popes of the last century and their more significant statements.

1. The Popes of the last century and Dante Alighieri

A hundred years ago, in 1921, Benedict XV commemorated the sixth centenary of the poet's death by issuing an Encyclical Letter[2] that made ample reference to earlier interventions by the Popes, particularly Leo XIII and Saint Pius X, and by encouraging the restoration of the Church of Saint Peter Major in Ravenna, popularly known as San Francesco, where Dante's funeral was celebrated and his remains were buried. The Pope expressed appreciation for the many initiatives undertaken to celebrate the anniversary and defended the right of

[2] *In Praeclara Summorum* (30 April 1921): AAS 13 (1921), 209-217.

the Church, "which was to him a mother", to take a leading role in those commemorations, honouring Dante as one of her children.[3] Previously, in a Letter to Archbishop Pasquale Morganti of Ravenna, Benedict XV had approved the programme of the centenary celebrations, adding that, "there is also a special reason why we deem that his solemn anniversary should be celebrated with grateful memory and broad participation: the fact that Alighieri is our own... Indeed, who can deny that our Dante nurtured and fanned the flame of his genius and poetic gifts by drawing inspiration from the Catholic faith, to such an extent that he celebrated the sublime mysteries of religion in a poem almost divine?".[4]

In a historical period marked by hostility to the Church, Pope Benedict reaffirmed the poet's fidelity to the Church, "the intimate union of Dante with this Chair of Peter". Indeed, he noted that the poet's work, while an expression of the "grandeur and keenness of his genius", drew "powerful

[3] Cf. ibid., 210.

[4] Letter *Nobis ad Catholicam* (28 October 1914): AAS 6 (1914), 540.

inspiration" precisely from the Christian faith. For this reason, the Pope continued, "we admire in him not only supreme height of genius but also the vastness of the subject that holy religion offered for his poetry". In extolling Dante, Benedict was responding indirectly to those who denied or criticized the religious inspiration of his work. "There breathes in Alighieri the devotion that we too feel; his faith resonates with ours… That is his great glory, to be a Christian poet, to have sung with almost divine notes those Christian ideals that he so passionately contemplated in all their splendour and beauty". Dante's work, the Pope stated, shows eloquently and effectively "how false it is to say that obedience of mind and heart to God is a hindrance to genius, which instead it spurs on and elevates". For this reason, the Pope continued, "the teachings bequeathed to us by Dante in all his works, but especially in his threefold poem", can serve "as a most precious guide for the men and women of our own time", particularly students and scholars, since "in composing his poem, Dante had no other purpose than to raise mortals from the state of misery, that is from the state of sin, and lead them to the state of happiness, that is of divine grace".

In 1965, for the seventh centenary of Dante's birth, Saint Paul VI intervened on a number of occasions. On 19 September that year, he donated a golden cross to adorn the shrine in Ravenna that preserves Dante's tomb, which previously had lacked "such a sign of religion and hope".[5] On 14 November, he sent a golden laurel wreath to Florence, to be mounted in the Baptistery of Saint John. Finally, at the conclusion of the Second Vatican Ecumenical Council, he wished to present the Council Fathers with an artistic edition of the Divine Comedy. Above all, however, Pope Paul honoured the memory of the great poet with an Apostolic Letter, *Altissimi Cantus*,[6] in which he reaffirmed the strong bond uniting the Church and Dante Alighieri. "There may be some who ask why the Catholic Church, by the will of its visible Head, is so concerned to cultivate the memory and celebrate the glory of the Florentine poet. Our response is easy: by special right, Dante is ours! Ours, by which we mean to say, of the Catholic

[5] *Address to the Sacred College and the Roman Prelature* (23 December 1965): AAS 58 (1966), 80.

[6] Cf. AAS 58 (1966), 22-37.

faith, for he radiated love for Christ; ours, because he loved the Church deeply and sang her glories; and ours too, because he acknowledged and venerated in the Roman Pontiff the Vicar of Christ".

Yet this right, the Pope added, far from justifying a certain triumphalism, also entails an obligation: "Dante is ours, we may well insist, but we say this not to treat him as a trophy for our own glorification, but to be reminded of our duty, in honouring him, to explore the inestimable treasures of Christian thought and sentiment present in his work. For we are convinced that only by better appreciating the religious spirit of the sovereign poet can we come to understand and savour more fully its marvellous spiritual riches". Nor does this obligation exempt the Church from accepting also the prophetic criticisms uttered by the poet with regard to those charged with proclaiming the Gospel and representing, not themselves, but Christ. "The Church does not hesitate to acknowledge that Dante spoke scathingly of more than one Pope, and had harsh rebukes for ecclesiastical institutions and for those who were representatives and ministers of the Church". All the same, it is clear that "such fiery attitudes never shook his firm Catholic faith and his filial affection for Holy Church".

Paul VI went on to illustrate what makes the Comedy a source of spiritual enrichment accessible to everyone. "Dante's poem is universal: in its immense scope, it embraces heaven and earth, eternity and time, divine mysteries and human events, sacred doctrine and teachings drawn from the light of reason, the fruits of personal experience and the annals of history". Above all, he stressed the intrinsic purpose of Dante's writings, and the Divine Comedy in particular, a purpose not always clearly appreciated or duly acknowledged. "The aim of the Divine Comedy is primarily practical and transformative. It seeks not only to be beautiful and morally elevating poetry, but to effect a radical change, leading men and women from chaos to wisdom, from sin to holiness, from poverty to happiness, from the terrifying contemplation of hell to the beatific contemplation of heaven".

Writing at a time of grave international tension, the Pope sought constantly to uphold the ideal of peace, and found in Dante's work a precious means for encouraging and sustaining that ideal. "The peace of individuals, families, nations and the human community, this peace internal and external, private and public, this tranquillity of order is disturbed and shaken because piety and justice are being trampled upon. To restore order and salvation, faith and reason, Beatrice and Virgil, the Cross and the Eagle, Church and Empire are called to operate in harmony". In this vein, he spoke of Dante's poem as a paean to peace. "The Divine Comedy is a poem of peace: the *Inferno* a dirge for peace forever lost, the *Purgatorio* a wistful hymn of hope for peace, and the *Paradiso* a triumphant anthem of peace fully and eternally possessed".

Viewed in this way, the Pope continued, the Comedy is "a poem of social improvement through the attainment of a freedom liberated from enslavement to evil and directed to the knowledge and love of God" and an expression of authentic humanism. "In Dante all human values – intellectual, moral, emotional, cultural and civic – are acknowledged and exalted. It should be noted, however, that this appreciation and esteem were the fruit of his deepening experience of the divine, as his contemplation was gradually purified of earthly elements". Rightly, therefore, could the Comedy be described as *Divine*, and Dante called the "supreme poet" and, in the opening words of the same Apostolic Letter, "the lord of sublime song".

In praising Dante's extraordinary artistic and literary gifts, Paul VI also restated a familiar principle. "Theology and philosophy are intrinsically related to beauty: to their teachings beauty lends its own vesture and adornment. Through music and the figurative and plastic arts, beauty opens a path that makes their lofty teachings accessible to many others. Erudite disquisitions and subtle reasoning are not easily understood by many people, yet they too hunger for the bread of truth. Attracted by beauty, they come to recognize and appreciate the light of truth and the fulfilment it brings. This is what the lord of sublime song understood and achieved; for him beauty became the handmaid of goodness and truth, and goodness a thing of beauty". Citing a line of the Comedy, Pope Paul concluded with the exhortation: "All honour be paid to the pre-eminent poet!" (*Inf.* IV, 80).

Saint John Paul II often referred to Dante in his addresses. Here, I would mention only that of 30 May 1985, for the inauguration of the exhibition *Dante in the Vatican*. Like Paul VI, he highlighted Dante's artistic genius, speaking of the poet's work as "a vision of reality that speaks of the life to come and the mystery of God with the vigour of theological thought transformed by the combined splendour of art and poetry". Pope John Paul reflected in particular on a key word from the Comedy: "*Trasumanare:* to pass beyond the human. This was Dante's ultimate effort: to ensure that the burden of what is human would not destroy the divine within us, nor that the greatness of the divine would cancel the value of what is human. For this reason the poet rightly interpreted his own personal history and that of all humanity in a theological key".

Benedict XVI frequently spoke of Dante's journey and from his poetry drew points for reflection and meditation. For example, in speaking of the theme of his first Encyclical Letter *Deus Caritas Est*, he began precisely from Dante's vision of God, in whom "light and love are one and the same", in order to emphasize the novelty found in Dante's work. "Dante perceives something completely new… the eternal light is shown in three circles which Dante addresses using those terse verses familiar to us: 'O Light Eterne, sole in thyself that dwellest, / Sole knowest thyself, and, known unto thyself, / And knowing, lovest and smilest upon thy self!' (*Par.* XXXIII, 124-126).

Indeed, even more impressive than this revelation of God as a Trinitarian circle of knowledge and love, is his discernment of a human face – the face of Jesus Christ – in the central circle of that light. God thus has a human face and – we might add – a human heart".[7] The Pope stressed the originality of Dante's vision, which gave poetic expression to the newness of the Christian experience: "the novelty of a love that moved God to take on a human face, and even more, to take on flesh and blood, our entire humanity".[8]

In my first Encyclical Letter *Lumen Fidei*,[9] I described the light of faith using an image drawn from the *Paradiso*, which speaks of that light as a "spark, / Which afterwards dilates to vivid flame, / And, like a star in heaven, is sparkling in me" (*Par.* XXIV, 145-147). I then commemorated the 750th anniversary of Dante's birth with a message, in which I expressed my hope that "the figure of

[7] *Address to Participants at the Meeting Promoted by the Pontifical Council "Cor Unum"*, 23 January 2006: *Insegnamenti* 2006 II/1, 92-93.

[8] Ibid., 93.

[9] Cf. No. 4: AAS 105 (2013), 557.

Alighieri and his work will be newly understood and appreciated". I proposed reading the Comedy as "an epic journey, indeed, a true pilgrimage, personal and interior, yet also communal, ecclesial, social and historical", inasmuch as "it represents the paradigm for every authentic journey whereby mankind is called to leave behind what the poet calls 'the threshing-floor that maketh us so proud' (*Par.* XXII, 151), in order to attain a new state of harmony, peace and happiness".[10] Dante can thus speak to the men and women of our own day as "a prophet of hope, a herald of the possibility of redemption, liberation and profound change for each individual and for humanity as a whole".[11]

More recently, on 10 October 2020, addressing a delegation from the Archdiocese of Ravenna-Cervia for the inauguration of the Year of Dante, I announced my intention to issue the present Letter. I noted that Dante's work can also enrich the minds and hearts of all those, especially the young who, once introduced to his poetry "in a way that is

[10] *Message to the President of the Pontifical Council for Culture* (4 May 2015): AAS 107 (2015), 551-552.

[11] Ibid., 552.

accessible to them, inevitably sense on the one hand a great distance from the author and his world, and yet on the other a remarkable resonance with their own experience".[12]

2. The life of Dante Alighieri: a paradigm of the human condition

With the present Apostolic Letter, I too would like to consider the life and work of the great poet and to explore its "resonance" with our own experience. I wish also to reaffirm its perennial timeliness and importance, and to appreciate the enduring warnings and insights it contains for humanity as a whole, not simply believers. Dante's work is an integral part of our culture, taking us back to the Christian roots of Europe and the West. It embodies that patrimony of ideals and values that the Church and civil society continue to propose as the basis of a humane social order in which all can and must see others as brothers and sisters. Without entering into the complex personal, political and judicial aspects of Dante's biography, I would briefly mention some events in his life that

[12] *L'Osservatore Romano*, 10 October 2020, p. 7.

make him appear remarkably close to many of our contemporaries and that remain essential for understanding his work.

Dante was born in 1265 in Florence and married Gemma Donati, who bore him four children. He remained deeply attached to his native city, despite the political disputes that in time caused him to be at odds with it. To the end he desired to return to Florence, not only because of his continued affection for his birthplace, but above all so that he could be crowned a poet where he had received baptism and the gift of faith (cf. *Par.* XXV, 1-9). In the headings of some of his *Letters* (III, V, VI and VII) Dante refers to himself as "*florentinus et exul inmeritus*", while in that addressed to Cangrande della Scala (XIII), he styles himself "*florentinus natione non moribus*".

A white Guelph, Dante found himself embroiled in the conflict between Guelphs and Ghibellines, and between white and black Guelphs. He held important public offices, including a term as Prior, but in 1302, as a result of political unrest, he was exiled for two years, banned from holding public office and sentenced to pay a fine. Dante rejected the decision as unjust, which only made his punishment more severe: perpetual exile, confiscation of his goods and a death sentence if he returned to Florence. This was the beginning of Dante's painful exile and his fruitless efforts to return to his native city, for which he had passionately fought.

He thus became an exile, a "pensive pilgrim" reduced to a state of "grievous poverty" (*Convivio*, I, III, 5). This led him to seek refuge and protection with various noble families, including the Scaligers of Verona and the Malaspina of Lunigiana. The words spoken by Cacciaguida, the poet's ancestor, capture something of the bitterness and despair of his new situation: "Thou shalt abandon everything beloved / Most tenderly, and this the arrow is / Which first the bow of banishment shoots forth. / Thou shalt have proof how savoureth of salt / The bread of others, and how hard a road / The going down and up another's stairs" (*Par.* XVII, 55-60).

In 1315, after refusing to accept the humiliating amnesty conditions that would have allowed him to return to Florence, Dante was once more sentenced to death, this time together with his adolescent children. His final place of exile was Ravenna, where he was hospitably received by Guido Novello da Polenta. There he died on the night between 13 and

14 September 1321, at the age of fifty-six, upon his return from a mission to Venice. His tomb was originally set into the outer wall of the old Franciscan cloister of Saint Peter Major, then relocated in 1865 to the adjacent eighteenth-century shrine which even today remains the goal of countless visitors and admirers of the great poet, the father of Italian language and literature.

In exile, Dante's love for Florence, betrayed by the "iniquitous Florentines" (*Ep.* VI, 1), was transformed into bittersweet nostalgia. His deep disappointment over the collapse of his political and civil ideals, together with his dreary wanderings from city to city in search of refuge and support are not absent from his literary and poetic work; indeed, they constitute its very source and inspiration. When Dante describes the pilgrims setting out for the holy places, he hints at his own state of mind and inmost feelings: "O pilgrims who make your way deep in thought..." (*Vita Nuova*, 29 [XL (XLI), 9], v. 1). This motif recurs frequently, as in the verse of the *Purgatorio*: "In the same way that thoughtful pilgrims do, / Who, unknown people on the road o'ertaking, / Turn themselves round to them, and do not stop" (XXIII, 16-18).

We can also see the poignant melancholy of Dante the pilgrim and exile in his celebrated verses of the eighth canto of the *Purgatorio*: "'Twas now the hour that turneth back desire / In those who sail the sea, and melts the heart, / The day they've said to their sweet friends farewell" (1-3).

Dante, pondering his life of exile, radical uncertainty, fragility, and constant moving from place to place, sublimated and transformed his personal experience, making it a paradigm of the human condition, viewed as a journey – spiritual and physical – that continues until it reaches its goal. Here two fundamental themes of Dante's entire work come to the fore, namely, that every existential journey begins with an innate desire in the human heart and that this desire attains fulfilment in the happiness bestowed by the vision of the Love who is God.

For all the tragic, sorrowful and distressing events he experienced, the great poet never surrendered or succumbed. He refused to repress his heart's yearning for fulfilment and happiness or to resign himself to injustice, hypocrisy, the arrogance of the powerful or the selfishness that turns our world into "the threshing-floor that maketh us so proud" (*Par.* XXII, 151).

3. The poet's mission as a prophet of hope

Reviewing the events of his life above all in the light of faith, Dante discovered his personal vocation and mission. From this, paradoxically, he emerged no longer an apparent failure, a sinner, disillusioned and demoralized, but a prophet of hope. In the Letter to Cangrande della Scala, he described with remarkable clarity the aim of his life's work, no longer pursued through political or military activity, but by poetry, the art of the word which, by speaking to all, has the power to change the life of each. "We must say briefly that the purpose of our whole work and its individual parts is to remove from their state of misery those who live this life and to lead them to a state of happiness" (XIII, 39 [15]). In this sense, it was meant to inspire a journey of liberation from every form of misery and human depravity (the "forest dark"), while at the same time pointing toward the ultimate goal of that journey: happiness, understood both as the fullness of life in time and history, and as eternal beatitude in God.

Dante thus became the herald, prophet and witness of this twofold end, this bold programme of life, and as such was confirmed in his mission by Beatrice: "Therefore, for that world's good which liveth ill, / Fix on the car thine eyes, and what thou seest, / Having returned to earth, take heed thou write" (*Purg.* XXXII, 103-105).

His ancestor Cacciaguida likewise urges him not to falter in his mission. After the poet briefly describes his journey in the three realms of the afterlife and acknowledges the dire consequences of proclaiming uncomfortable or painful truths, his illustrious forebear replies: "A conscience overcast / Or with its own or with another's shame, / Will taste forsooth the tartness of thy word; / But ne'ertheless, all falsehood laid aside, / Make manifest thy vision utterly, / And let them scratch wherever is the itch" (*Par.* XVII, 124-129).

Saint Peter likewise encourages Dante to embark courageously upon his prophetic mission. The Apostle, following a bitter invective against Boniface VIII, tells the poet: "And thou, my son, who by thy mortal weight / Shalt down return again, open thy mouth; / What I conceal not, do not thou conceal" (*Par.* XXVII, 64-66).

Dante's prophetic mission thus entailed denouncing and criticizing those believers – whether Popes or the ordinary faithful – who betray Christ and turn the Church into a means for advancing their own interests while ignoring the spirit of the Beatitudes and the duty of charity towards the defenceless and poor, and instead idolizing power and riches: "For whatsoever hath the Church in keeping / Is for the folk that ask it in God's name / Not for one's kindred or for something worse" (*Par.* XXII, 82-84).

Yet, even as he denounces corruption in parts of the Church, Dante also becomes – through the words of Saint Peter Damian, Saint Benedict and Saint Peter – an advocate for her profound renewal and implores God's providence to bring this about: "But the high Providence, that with Scipio / At Rome the glory of the world defended, / Will speedily bring aid, as I conceive" (*Par.* XXVII, 61-63).

Dante the exile, the pilgrim, powerless yet confirmed by the profound interior experience that had changed his life, was reborn as a result of the vision that, from the depths of hell, from the ultimate degradation of our humanity, elevated him to the very vision of God. He thus emerged as the herald of a new existence, the prophet of a new humanity that thirsts for peace and happiness.

4. Dante as the poet of human desire

Dante reads the depths of the human heart. In everyone, even in the most abject and disturbing figures, he can discern a spark of the desire to attain some measure of happiness and fulfilment. He stops and listens to the souls he meets; he converses with them and questions them, and thus identifies with them and shares in their torments or their bliss. Starting from his own personal situation, Dante becomes the interpreter of the universal human desire to follow the journey of life to its ultimate destination, when the fullness of truth and the answers to life's meaning will be revealed and, in the words of Saint Augustine,[13] our hearts find their rest and peace in God.

In the *Convivio,* Dante analyses the dynamism of desire: "The ultimate desire of every being, and the first bestowed by nature, is the desire to return to its first cause. And since God is the first cause of our souls... the soul desires first and foremost to return

[13] Cf. *Confessions*, I, I, 1: PL 32, 661.

to him. Like a pilgrim who travels an unknown road and believes every house he sees is the hostel, and upon finding that it is not, transfers this belief to the next house he sees, and the next, and the next, until at last he arrives at the hostel, so it is with our souls. As soon as it sets out on the new and untravelled road of this life, the soul incessantly seeks its supreme good; consequently, whenever it sees something apparently good, it considers that the supreme good" (IV, XII, 14-15).

Dante's journey, especially as it appears in the Divine Comedy, was truly a journey of desire, of a deep interior resolve to change his life, to discover happiness and to show the way to others who, like him, find themselves in a "forest dark" after losing "the right way". It is significant that, at the very start of this journey, his guide – the great Latin poet Virgil – points to its goal and urges him not to succumb to fear or fatigue: "But thou, why goest thou back to such annoyance? / Why climb'st thou not the Mount Delectable, / Which is the source and cause of every joy?" (*Inf.* I, 76-78).

5. The poet of God's mercy and human freedom

The journey that Dante presents is not illusory or utopian; it is realistic and within the reach of everyone, for God's mercy always offers the possibility of change, conversion, new self-awareness and discovery of the path to true happiness. Significant in this regard are several episodes and individuals in the Comedy which show that no one on earth is precluded from this path. There is the emperor Trajan, a pagan who nonetheless is placed in heaven. Dante justifies his presence thus: "*Regnum coelorum* suffereth violence / From fervent love, and from that living hope / That overcometh the Divine volition; / Not in the guise that man o'ercometh man / But conquers it because it will be conquered / And conquered conquers by benignity" (*Par.* XX, 94-99).

Trajan's gesture of charity towards a "poor widow" (45), or the "little tear" of repentance shed at the point of death by Buonconte di Montefeltro (*Purg.* V, 107), are not only signs of God's infinite mercy, but also confirm that human beings remain ever free to choose which path to follow and which destiny to embrace.

Significant too is King Manfred, placed by Dante in Purgatory, who thus describes his death and God's judgement: "After I had my body lacerated / By these two mortal stabs, I gave myself / Weeping to Him, who willingly doth pardon. / Horrible my iniquities had been; / But Infinite Goodness hath such ample arms / That it receives whatever turns to it" (*Purg.* III, 118-123).

Here we can almost glimpse the father in the Gospel parable who welcomes with open arms the return of his prodigal son (cf. *Lk* 15:11-32).

Dante champions the dignity and freedom of each human being as the basis for decisions in life and for faith itself. Our eternal destiny – so Dante suggests by recounting the stories of so many individuals great and small – depends on our free decisions. Even our ordinary and apparently insignificant actions have a meaning that transcends time: they possess an eternal dimension. The greatest of God's gifts is the freedom that enables us to reach our ultimate goal, as Beatrice tells us: "The greatest gift that in his largess God / Creating made, and unto his own goodness / Nearest conformed, and that which he doth prize / Most highly, is the freedom of the will" (*Par.* V, 19-22).

These are not vague rhetorical statements, for they spring from the lives of men and women who knew the cost of freedom: "He seeketh Liberty, which is so dear / As knoweth he who life for her refuses" (*Purg.* I, 71-72).

Freedom, Dante reminds us, is not an end unto itself; it is a condition for rising constantly higher. His journey through the three kingdoms vividly illustrates this ascent, which ultimately reaches heaven and the experience of utter bliss. The "profound desire" (*Par.* XXII, 61) awakened by freedom is not sated until it attains its goal, the final vision and the blessedness it brings: "And I, who to the end of all desires / Was now approaching, even as I ought / The ardour of desire within me ended" (*Par.* XXXIII, 46-48).

Desire thus becomes prayer, supplication, intercession and song accompanying and marking Dante's journey, just as liturgical prayer marks the hours and moments of the day. The poet's paraphrase of the *Our Father* (cf. *Purg.* XI, 1-21) intertwines the Gospel text with all the hardships and sufferings of daily experience: "Come unto us the peace of thy dominion / For unto it we cannot of ourselves… / Give unto us this day our daily manna / Without which in this rough wilderness / Backward goes he who toils most to advance" (7-8, 13-15).

The freedom of those who believe in God as a merciful Father can only be offered back to him in prayer. Nor does this detract in the least from that freedom; it only strengthens it.

6. The image of man in the vision of God

Throughout the journey of the Comedy, as Pope Benedict XVI noted, the interplay of freedom and desire does not entail, as one might think, a diminution of our concrete humanity or a kind of self-alienation; it does not destroy or disregard our historicity. In the *Paradiso*, Dante represents the blessed – the "white stoles" (XXX, 129) – in their bodily form, portraying their affections and emotions, their glances and their gestures; in a word, he shows us humanity in its ultimate perfection of soul and body, prefiguring the resurrection of the flesh. Saint Bernard, who accompanies Dante on the last stretch of the journey, points out to the poet the presence of small children in the rose of the blessed; he tells him to watch them and to listen to their voices: "Well canst thou recognise it in their faces / And also in their voices puerile / If thou regard them well and hearken to them" (XXXII, 46-48).

It is touching to think that the luminous presence of the blessed in their full humanity is motivated not only by their affection for their loved ones, but above all by the explicit desire once more to see their bodies, their earthly features: "That well they showed desire for their dead bodies; / Nor sole for them perhaps, but for the mothers, / The fathers, and the rest who had been dear / Or ever they became eternal flames" (XIV, 63-66).

Finally, at the centre of the final vision, in his encounter with the mystery of the Blessed Trinity, Dante descries a human face, the face of Christ, the eternal Word made flesh in the womb of Mary: "Within the deep and luminous subsistence / Of the High Light appeared to me three circles / Of threefold colour and of one dimension… / That circulation, which being thus conceived / Appeared in thee as a reflected light / When somewhat contemplated by mine eyes / Within itself, of its own very colour / Seemed to me painted with our effigy" (XXXIII, 115-117, 127-131).

Only in the *visio Dei* does our human desire attain fulfilment and our arduous journey come to its end: "my mind there smote / A flash of lightning, wherein came its wish / Here vigour failed the lofty fantasy" (140-142).

The mystery of the incarnation, which we celebrate today, is the true heart and inspiration of the entire poem. For it effected what the Fathers of the Church call our "divinization", the *admirabile commercium*, the prodigious exchange whereby God enters our history by becoming flesh, and humanity, in its flesh, is enabled to enter the realm of the divine, symbolized by the rose of the blessed. Our humanity, in its concreteness, with our daily gestures and words, with our intelligence and affections, with our bodies and emotions, is taken up into God, in whom it finds true happiness and ultimate fulfilment, the goal of all its journeying. Dante had desired and looked forward to this goal at the beginning of the *Paradiso*: "More the desire should be enkindled in us / That essence to behold, wherein is seen / How God and our own nature were united. / There will be seen what we receive by faith, / Not demonstrated, but self-evident / In guise of the first truth that man believes" (II, 40-45).

7. The three women of the Comedy: Mary, Beatrice and Lucy

In celebrating the mystery of the incarnation, the source of salvation and joy for all humanity, Dante cannot but sing the praises of Mary, the Virgin Mother who, by her *fiat*, her full and total acceptance of God's plan, enabled the Word to become flesh.

In Dante's work, we find a splendid treatise of Mariology. With sublime lyricism, particularly in the prayer of Saint Bernard, the poet synthesizes theology's reflection on the figure of Mary and her participation in the mystery of God: "Thou Virgin Mother, daughter of thy Son, / Humble and high beyond all other creature, / The limit fixed of the eternal counsel, / Thou art the one who such nobility / To human nature gave, that its Creator / Did not disdain to make himself its creature" (*Par.* XXXIII, 1-6).

The opening oxymoron and the subsequent flood of contrasts celebrate the uniqueness of Mary and her singular beauty.

Pointing to the blessed arrayed in the mystical rose, Saint Bernard invites Dante to contemplate Mary, who gave a human face to the Incarnate Word: "Look now into the face that unto Christ / Hath most resemblance; for its brightness only / Is able to prepare thee to see Christ" (*Par.* XXXII, 85-87).

The mystery of the Incarnation is again evoked by the presence of the Archangel Gabriel. Dante questions Saint Bernard: "Who is the Angel that with so much joy / Into the eyes is looking of our Queen, /

Enamoured so that he seems made of fire?" (103-105).

To which Bernard responds: "he is the one who bore the palm / Down unto Mary, when the Son of God / To take our burden on himself decreed" (112-114).

References to Mary abound in the Divine Comedy. In the *Purgatorio*, at every step of the way she embodies the virtues opposed to the vices; she is the morning star who helps the poet to emerge from the dark forest and to seek the mountain of God; the invocation of her name, "The name of that fair flower I e'er invoke / Morning and evening…" (*Par.* XXIII, 88-89), prepares the pilgrim for the encounter with Christ and the mystery of God.

Dante is never alone on his journey. He lets himself be guided, first by Virgil, a symbol of human reason, and then by Beatrice and Saint Bernard. Now, through the intercession of Mary, he can rise to our heavenly homeland and taste in its fullness the joy that had been his life-long desire: "and distilleth yet / Within my heart the sweetness born of it" (*Par.* XXXIII, 62-63).

We are not saved alone, the poet seems to repeat, conscious of his need: "I come not of myself" (*Inf.* X, 61).

The journey needs to be made in the company of another, who can support us and guide us with wisdom and prudence.

Here we see how significant is the presence of women in the poem. At the beginning of Dante's arduous journey, Virgil, his first guide, comforts and encourages Dante to persevere because three women are interceding for him and will guide his steps: Mary, the Mother of God, representing charity; Beatrice, representing hope; and Saint Lucy, representing faith. Beatrice is introduced in the poignant verses: "Beatrice am I, who do bid thee go; / I come from there, where I would fain return; / Love moved me, which compelleth me to speak" (*Inf.* II, 70-72).

Love thus appears as the sole means of our salvation, the divine love that transfigures human love. Beatrice speaks in turn of the intercession of yet another woman, the Virgin Mary: "A gentle Lady is in Heaven, who grieves / At this impediment, to which I send thee, / So that stern judgment there above is broken" (94-96).

Lucy then intervenes, addressing Beatrice: "Beatrice,… the true praise of God, / Why succourest thou not him, who loved thee so, / For thee he issued from the vulgar herd?" (103-105).

Dante recognizes that only one moved by love can truly support us on the journey and bring us to salvation, to renewed life and thus to happiness.

8. Francis, the spouse of Lady Poverty

In the pure white rose of the blessed, with Mary as its radiant centre, Dante places a number of saints whose life and mission he describes. He presents them as men and women who, in the concrete events of life and despite many trials, achieved the ultimate purpose of their life and vocation. Here I will mention only Saint Francis of Assisi, as portrayed in Canto XI of the *Paradiso*, the sphere of the wise.

Saint Francis and Dante had much in common. Francis, with his followers, left the cloister and went out among the people, in small towns and the streets of the cities, preaching to them and visiting their homes. Dante made the choice, unusual for that age, to compose his great poem on the afterlife in the vernacular, and to populate his tale with characters both famous and obscure, yet equal in dignity to the rulers of this world. Another feature common to the two was their sensitivity to the beauty and worth of creation as the reflection and imprint of its Creator. We can hardly fail to hear in Dante's paraphrase of the *Our Father* an echo of Saint Francis's *Canticle of the Sun*: "Praised be thy name and thine omnipotence / By every creature… " (*Purg.* XI, 4-5).

In Canto XI of the *Paradiso*, this comparison becomes even more pronounced. The sanctity and wisdom of Francis stand out precisely because Dante, gazing from heaven upon the earth, sees the crude vulgarity of those who trust in earthly goods: "O Thou insensate care of mortal men, / How inconclusive are the syllogisms / That make thee beat thy wings in downward flight!" (1-3).

The entire history of Saint Francis, his "admirable life", revolved around his privileged relationship with Lady Poverty: "But that too darkly I may not proceed, / Francis and Poverty for these two lovers / Take thou henceforward in my speech diffuse" (73-75).

The canto of Saint Francis recalls the salient moments of his life, his trials and ultimately the moment when his configuration to Christ, poor and crucified, found its ultimate divine confirmation in his reception of the stigmata: "And, finding for conversion too unripe / The folk, and not to tarry there in vain, / Returned to fruit of the Italic grass, / On the rude rock 'twixt Tiber and the Arno / From Christ did he receive the final seal, / Which during two whole years his members bore" (103-108).

9. Accepting the testimony of Dante Alighieri

At the conclusion of this brief glance at Dante Alighieri's work, an almost inexhaustible mine of knowledge, experience and thought in every field of human research, we are invited to reflect on its significance. The wealth of characters, stories, symbols and evocative images that the poet sets before us certainly awakens our admiration, wonder and gratitude. In Dante we can almost glimpse a forerunner of our multimedia culture, in which word and image, symbol and sound, poetry and dance converge to convey a single message. It is understandable, then, that his poem has inspired the creation of countless works of art in every genre.

But the work of the supreme poet also raises provocative questions for our own times. What can he communicate to us in this day and age? Does he still have anything to say to us or offer us? Is his message relevant or useful to us? Can it still challenge us?

Dante today – if we can presume to speak for him – does not wish merely to be read, commented on, studied and analyzed. Rather, he asks to be heard and even imitated; he invites us to become his companions on the journey. Today, too, he wants to show us the route to happiness, the right path to live a fully human life, emerging from the dark forest in which we lose our bearings and the sense of our true worth. Dante's journey and his vision of life beyond death are not just a story to be told; they are more than the account of a personal experience, however exceptional.

If Dante tells his tale admirably, using the language of the people yet elevating it to a universal language, it is because he has an important message to convey, one meant to touch our hearts and minds, to transform and change us even now, in this present life. A message that can and should make us appreciate fully who we are and the meaning of our daily struggles to achieve happiness, fulfilment and our ultimate end, our true homeland, where we will be in full communion with God, infinite and eternal Love. Dante was a man of his time, with sensibilities different from ours in certain areas, yet his humanism remains timely and relevant, a sure reference point for what we hope to accomplish in our own day.

It is fitting, then, that the present anniversary serve as an incentive to make Dante's work better known and appreciated, accessible and attractive, not only to students and scholars but to all those who seek answers to their deepest questions and wish to live their lives to the full, purposefully undertaking their own journey of life and faith, with gratitude for the gift and responsibility of freedom.

I express my deep appreciation, then, to those teachers who passionately communicate Dante's message and introduce others to the cultural, religious and moral riches contained in his works. Yet this great heritage cries out to be made accessible beyond the halls of schools and universities.

I urge Christian communities, especially in cities associated with Dante's life, academic institutions and cultural associations to promote initiatives aimed at making better known his message in all its fullness.

In a special way, I encourage artists to give voice, face and heart, form, colour and sound to Dante's poetry by following the path of beauty which he so masterfully travelled. And thus to communicate the most profound truths and to proclaim, in the language of their art, a message of peace, freedom and fraternity.

At this particular moment in history, overclouded by situations of profound inhumanity and a lack of confidence and prospects for the future, the figure of Dante, prophet of hope and witness to the human desire for happiness, can still provide us with words and examples that encourage us on our journey. Dante can help us to advance with serenity and courage on the pilgrimage of life and faith that each of us is called to make, until our hearts find true peace and true joy, until we arrive at the ultimate goal of all humanity:

"The Love which moves the sun and the other stars" (*Par.* XXXIII, 145).

From the Vatican, on 25 March, the Solemnity of the Annunciation of the Lord, in the year 2021, the ninth of my Pontificate.

Franciscus

INDEX

www.ingramcontent.com/pod-product-compliance
Ingram Content Group UK Ltd.
Pitfield, Milton Keynes, MK11 3LW, UK
UKHW021643190726
13853UKWH00001B/16

9 788826 606163